MOMENTS

OF

BEAUTY

POEMS BY

UKU BROWN

Copyright © 2024 Uku Brown

All rights reserved. No part of this book may be reproduced, stored in a retrieval system in any form or by any means, electronic, mechanical, photocopying, recording, or otherwise, without written permission of the publisher, except where permitted by law.
To request permissions, contact the publisher at info@aconscioustide.com

aconscioustide.com

TABLE OF CONTENTS

Dedication	7
Introduction	8

POETRY

1. The winkstress	9
2. Friends	12
3. Lets build a house	16
4. We never wear our bodies	18
5. Black Swan	21
6. I will call you my beautiful flame	26
7. I will cry your tears	27
8. Would you like to fall apart in my arms	28
9. Everything comes through you	31
10. We washed our minds with stars	33

TABLE OF CONTENTS CONT..

POETRY

11. Where are you now	34
12. Keepers of the fire	37
13. Keepers of the fire part 2	39
14. I love your eyes	40
15. So many tears	42
16. Between your love and my death	44
17. Do not fear the darkness	47
18. I hear the waves are calling	50
19. Share your food	53
20. Too much love	55

TABLE OF CONTENTS CONT..

POETRY

21. Jupiter	56
22. Last lonely sleep	58
23. Big disco in the sky	61
24. Soft fire	64
25. Dream lovers	66
26. Oh my darling	68
27. I don't mind	70
28. Salt blue sea	72
29. Colours and sounds	75
30. I love you bird	77

From The Author

DEDICATION

Dedicated to the beautiful dreamers of peace, the observers of wonder, the quiet ones, the trees and the stars, the energy unseen that moves through all things inside an invisible mist of feminine cooperation, in a symbiotic dance of light and dark and pulsing with love. The joy, the sorrow, the love, my children and their mothers and all children and all mothers and the great mother of us all

INTRODUCTION

Some of these poems are songs and some of these songs are poems. Some have surfaced in tracks by the moonflowers, solar mumuns, the phoenix family and invisible pair of hands. I am very grateful to those collaborators and sonic adventurers and I send love to you all.

. Like burs from the burdock plant these poems have stuck to me and have now fallen onto these pages to share with you.

Like for many it can be a struggle sometimes to keep the wolf from the door. Whilst in my heart I know there's a joy to be shared in a single drop of dew that a thousand kings could never buy and that true wealth and beauty are honored with a free heart

Let's not fear the beauty, let's embrace it, we know that great joy and sadness lay there. Let's not hold on to it, but let it hold us. Let's not give it a name or a colour, let it be free, let it choose us as we volunteer to love.

I

THE WINKSTRESS

The winkstress wakes
in the sleepy light of morning
yawning still
transfixed with night
holding to the last kiss of
darkness
hear her sigh
she signals life

THE WINKSTRESS CONT...

Her limbs are new
and a little awkward
she had wings
in her dream for flight
she was to pass through
the silver moonbeams
but she awoke
with the morning's light

SHE WAS TO PASS THROUGH SILVER MOONBEAMS.

2
FRIENDS

i have a friend
she is the sea
she counts waves home
at night
and when they are
all safely home
she lets them all back out

i have a friend
she is the wind
she blows around the place
and in the morning
as i awake
she blows upon my face

'SHE COUNTS WAVES HOME AT NIGHT.'

FRIENDS CONT..

i have a friend, they are the sun.
they shine on us today.
i can't always see them
when they are there,
but I know
when they go away.

i have a friend,
she is the moon.
she shines both bright and bare.
she plays with the water
in my body
and makes my blood go dark.

FRIENDS CONT..

i have a friend

she is the earth

i will lay with her tonight

shes been my lover

all my time

and to all things

she brings life

3

LETS BUILD A HOUSE

Let's build a house
by the edge of the sea
in a magic forest
and quiet as a mouse
we will watch the tide out
from a tower
built by dreamers

we'll know the night
and we'll be friends
with all its
starry riches

therl be no time
just moments of beauty
endlessly touching

AND QUIET AS A MOUSE
WE'LL WATCH THE TIDE OUT
FROM A TOWER BUILT BY DREAMERS

4
WE NEVER WEAR OUR BODIES
(WHEN OUR MINDS ARE FREE)

Strange is the way a flame will dance

in a windy room

strange like the waves in the sky

that bring my heart to you

strange like the moon

when it bleeds it's tears

of joy and sadness

strange like your eyes

with no colour or pain

i fall into your laughter

and I fall in through your skin

and we fall into the space

where our bodies had been

but we never wear our bodies

when our minds are free

WE NEVER WEAR OUR BODIES
(WHEN OUR MINDS ARE FREE)CONT..

Strange like two rivers

two seas

and two dreams

strange like the colours of darkness

that wash our bodies clean

Strange like the corn

that shakes with out tears

strange like our loves

never ending or beginning

as we flow across the land

carrying seeds

WE NEVER WEAR OUR BODIES (WHEN OUR MINDS ARE FREE)CONT..

Strange like the angels

that touch us

as we melt into ether

strange we are gone and here

and sleeping with all softness

like leaves we shake and fall.....

into your laughter

and i fall in through your skin

WE FALL INTO THE SPACE
WHERE OUR BODIES HAD BEEN

5
THE BLACK SWAN

Where the Black swan goes to cry
we will meet my love and lie
on a bed of yellow lilies
we will wash ourselves
with tears
till our soft light's
at its strongest
between our night and day
without fear without conflict
we will fall into the water

we will run into one another
flow down into the ocean
and then we'll rise again as clouds
fly across the mountains
till we reach the tree of dreams
where we will
rest beneath her branches
and watch the
seven seasons turn

WHERE THE BLACK SWAN GOES TO CRY
WE WILL MEET MY LOVE AND LAY

THE BLACK SWAN..CONT..

Where the Black swan goes to cry
we will meet my love and lie
on a bed of yellow lilies
we will wash ourselves
with tears
till our soft light's
at it's strongest
between our night and day
with out fear without conflict
we will fall into the water

And dance amongst
the hidden lights
beneath the waves of love
where the tears of joy
and sadness wait
for every girl and boy
till the sun shones out the water
and the moon falls down like rain
we will wait beneath
the waves of love
to keep all their tears safe

WHERE THE TEARS OF
JOY AND SADNESS WAIT
FOR EVERY GIRL AND BOY

6
I WILL CALL YOU MY BEAUTIFUL FLAME

If you run away
i will not follow
if you hide away
i will not seek
but if you lay down
i will cover you in roses
and if you call my name
i will not sleep

when you wake in the morning
i will kiss you
with a smile upon my face
and with the light of the morning
upon your skin
i will call you my beautiful flame

oh beautiful flame
burning softly
with our love
we will go to the sea

IF YOU CALL MY NAME
I WILL NOT SLEEP

7
I'LL CRY YOUR TEARS

dont you cry now
i will do it for you
i never could
all these years

just sit down
you can watch me
just sit down
i will cry your tears

8
WOULD YOU LIKE TO FALL APART IN MY ARMS

would you like to
fall apart in my arms
we'll share our love
to keep us strong

well share the night
and all of its charms
and when we wake
there we will be

for the waves of love are strong
we'll let our ship be swept along
we'll use our arms like wings or fins
and where theres love
we'll jump in

FOR THE WAVES OF LOVE ARE STRONG

WOULD YOU LIKE TO FALL APART IN MY ARMS CONT..

would you like to
fall apart in my arms
we'll share our love
to keep us warm
we'll share the night
and all of its charms
and when we wake
there we will be

just you and me

EVERYTHING COMES THROUGH YOU

everything comes through you
you do not take
everything comes through you
you do not take
life makes you dance on graves
waves make you bend and shake
everything comes through you
you do not take

LIFE MAKES YOU DANCE ON GRAVES

WE WASHED OUR MINDS WITH STARS

we washed our minds

with stars

from worlds so far

and ran

into the sea

to breathe

11
WHERE ARE YOU NOW

where are you now

with the stars

in your eyes

*i've been watching the tide
and I almost went blind*

where are you now

with the stars

in your eyes

*i've been watching the sky
it helps me keep time*

WHERE ARE YOU NOW CONT...

where are you now
with the stars
in your eyes

*i've been blown by the wind
and it blow me right here*

where are you now
with the stars
in your eyes

*i've been waiting for the night to come
and stand by my side*

I'VE BEEN WAITING FOR THE NIGHT TO COME
AND STAND BY MY SIDE

12
THE KEEPERS OF THE FIRE

each fire is a star on earth

a reflection of the universe

a childs cry

a scream for reconition

a sacrifice for love

a dream for the dreamers

of a world lost to time

the flames show our passion

that burns deep inside

the heat cooks our bones

and the love

that we find

whilst the fire sings songs

in a whispering tone

that helps us remember

before we were born

WE BURN FLAMES FOR THE STARS
TO SHOW THEM WE'RE ALIVE

THE KEEPERS OF THE FIRE
PART 2

we, we have met in flames

and when we meet again

we will meet in love

we, we have met in dreams

i swam a river through your eyes

and dreams they can come true

we, we have met in music

music is like love

except we do not touch

we are the keepers

of the fire

we burn flames for the stars

to show them

we are alive

I LOVE YOUR EYES

i love your eyes
they're dark and know of magic
i love the way that they look
do they see me

i love your lips
i love the shapes that they take
i love the noises they make
will they kiss me

THEY'RE DARK
AND KNOW OF MAGIC

15
SO MANY TEARS

There are so many tears to cry
who's going to cry them
there are so many dreams to fade
whose going to fade them
there are so many hearts to break
who's going to break them

in this world so full of tears
we ought to share a little love
it may all disappear
for the worlds hanging on
by a silver thread
we ought to
share a little love
it's what everyone needs

SO MANY TEARS CONT...

there are so many tears to cry
who's going to cry them
there's so many homes to bomb
who's going to bomb them
there are so many children going to die
who's going to kill them
there are so many lives to lose
who's going to lose them

in this world so full of greed
we ought to share a little love
it's what everyone needs
for the world is hanging on by a silver thread
we ought to share a little love
it may all disappear
For there's only love and fear
we ought to share a little love
it might all disappear

16

BETWEEN YOUR LOVE AND MY DEATH

i can hear you calling me
between the waves of time
between the land and tide
between your love and my death

i can hear you calling me
between the waves of time
between the land and tide
between your love and my death

BETWEEN YOUR LOVE AND MY DEATH
WE'LL WATCH THE SHIPS GET WRECKED

BETWEEN YOUR LOVE AND MY DEATH CONT....

i can hear you calling me
from the rocks above my hand
i can feel you next to me
i can feel the ecstasy

between your love and my death
we can watch the ships get wrecked
between the lost and the found
we can watch them run aground

calling me home again
softly calling me home again
between your love and my death

17
DO NOT FEAR THE DARKNESS

Do not fear the darkness
in her claw breathes sanity
in there there is calmness
and in all things we cannot see

In my dreams I fought a giant
who passed through walls of steel
not the good king of the fire
came for me
but I would not go
i want to live my life

My love is her own
and together
we have flown
we struck a dagger through the eye
of all the creatures of the throne

DO NOT FEAR THE DARKNESS CONT...

In another i scanned the world
for shells and other jewels like rocks
to put inside of my glass box
in which my lover lay
she loved too much

Like all the beggars
that you see
their only crime
is their honesty

And if you find me in a ditch
with my blood
green and stagnent
and my flesh has turned to puss
a passing beggar will say of me
here lays a man
whom loved .... too much

IN MY DREAMS
I FOUGHT A GIANT.

I HEAR THE WAVES ARE CALLING

take me to the river
that flows down to the sea
i hear the waves are waiting
i hear the waves are waiting
i hear the waves are waiting
for me

sail me down the river
i'd like to go with you
i know your boat is leaving
i know your boat is leaving
i know your boat is leaving
and id like to go with you

I HEAR THE WAVES ARE CALLING CONT...

and when we get down to the sea
we must find our own way
but as long as there are stars above
as long as there are stars above
as long as there are stars
our love will find away

i can here the waves are calling
and know that your boat is leaving
but as long as there are stars above
our love will find away

AS LONG AS THERE ARE STARS ABOVE
OUR LIVE WILL FIND AWAY

SHARE YOUR FOOD

We are little twigs

on the edges of a small branch

to smaller creatures

we are home

we drop our seeds

like rain

let's hope they find good earth

our leaves

will form a shelter

from above

and each year we will grow

to soon becomes a forest

where no hungry creature roams

we will each be our own master

and not be our own slave

we will learn to grow together

every day

share your food

EACH YEAR WE WILL GROW
TILL SOON BECOMES A FOREST

TOO MUCH LOVE

if you feel like
you have too much love
inside your body
like you've the world
inside your breast
just put on sweet soul music
and let the magic
do the rest

you might be lucky
and if your spirit is ready
then your heart can
visit a place of rest

if you feel like
youve too much love in your body

 **21**

JUPITER

Away we will sail
on a boat built by our hands
we must leave this bad land
we've been told by the whales

The whales will follow
on our way to a new life
we will be their children
they will be our tomorrow

We'll leave no land crying
on our way to Jupiter
and if we don't get there
then we will die trying

WE'LL BE THEIR CHILDREN

THE LAST LONELY SLEEP

They say the wind blows
but I know she sucks
she sucks out
the trees
and the dreams
and the rocks

The young
they will bend
and shake their way out
but the old
they will crack
and fall with a shout

THE LAST LONELY SLEEP CONT..

And the love
will be lost
and she sings as she sleeps
the times past to weep
the times here to sleep
the last lonely sleep

And she says without store
all beauty will die
all beauty will fall

She lays down to die
with the last tear in her eye
the last kiss on her lips
the last song on her tongue
the last wind in her breath
the last star in her eye
all beauty will fall
all beauty......will die

THE LAST LONELY SLEEP

23

THE BIG DISCO IN THE SKY

Another friend died today
although a soft star
she shone for everyone
and never had a bad word
for anyone
I wish she'd stayed

A wild wide-eyed girl
with a glimmer of sadness
like that which befalls anyone
who can't understand
why people don't show
their beauty on the outside
and live their lives in peace

THE BIG DISCO IN THE SKY CONT...

I guess she was just
on earth on holiday
and never really lived here
anyway

So what else is there to say
as another angel
with delicate wings
falls in the storm

See you in the big disco in the sky
and thank you

SEE YOU IN THE BIG DISCO
IN THE SKY

SOFT FIRE

We walked beside a soft fire
Our limbs were warmed and gentle
My heart was beating in your hand
Your heart was beating through the land

Like the breath
That leaves the morning dew
Like the light that shines from you

And we melt into the soft fire

And we dance into the soft fire

And we dance into the soft fire

Like the light that shines from you

We dance into the fire

Like the light that shines from you

YOUR HEART WAS BEATING
THROUGH THE LAND

 25

DREAM LOVERS

you and i are different planets

but alike inside

equal distance from the sun

but when I fall you rise

we are not like

other lovers

we are far from earth

watch our comets

as they collided

light up the sky

and universe

YOU AND I
ARE DIFFERENT PLANETS
BUT ALIKE INSIDE

26
OH MY DARLING

oh my darling
you be free
like the water
in the breeze
like the water in the sea
be free
and run to me

oh my darling
you be free
like the moonlight
in the trees
like the water
in the sea
be free
and run to me

OH MY DARLING CONT...

oh my darling

you be free

like

like the sun that shines on water

like the drops of morning dew

then i will be free

to run to you

27
I DON'T MIND

i was waking
from a soft and gentle sleep
i'd been dreaming
that i walked beside a dream
i saw water
as a passing and wise being
on it's journey
to the sea and everything

oh and i don't mind the sun
and i don't mind the rain
and i don't mind walking
with the wind on my face

I DON'T MIND CONT...

i stood looking
about at everything
and I could see
it was looking back at me
I was hearing
a voice made out of light
I was held
and everything was right
i was floating
on my way down to the sea
and then I saw
the stream was me

oh and i don't mind the sun
and i don't mind the rain
and i don't mind walking
with the wind on my face

28
COLOURS AND SOUNDS

i am a man
with many friends
natural and real
from the world of plants and animals
spirits and people
it comes in the shape of water
and the colour of the air
it's in the things that the wind brings
as it scatters round the earth

at times the world's without
at times the world's within
like moments of death and birth
from worlds we are passing
for Rosemary and Abigale
one has come and one has gone
the world still turns
the sun still shines
and life goes on and on

COLOURS AND SOUNDS CONT...

We could fly away
and never look back
leave the world
to spin silently
in its suicide pact

and all the colours and sounds
that pass through us in space
will fall down
to the earth
and put a
smile on her face

ALL THE COLOURS AND SOUNDS
THAT PASS THROUGH US IN SPACE
WILL FALL DOWN TO THE EARTH AND
PUT A SMILE ON HER FACE

29
SALT BLUE SEA

oh the sailor he smiled
as he said to me
i must return to the salt blue sea
to heal my wounds
and set myself free
i must return to the salt blue sea

for the love
ive lost
and the love ive found
the love ive saved
and the love ive drowned
the love ive held
and the love ive crowned
the love thats up
and the love thats down

SALT BLUE SEA CONT..

oh the sailor he smiled
as he said to me
i must return to the salt blue sea
to heal my wounds
and set myself free
i must return to the salt blue sea

30
I LOVE YOU BIRD

Shafts of light
pierce my brain and heart
purple green and gold
like the sun
warm sharp
deadly life sharp
more than words can dream sharp

Then the softness
glowing moving after colours
kissing me all over
all my skin and more
surrounding me
inside me

I LOVE YOU BIRD CONT...

Then the white waves come
brilliant white
and full of stars
washing me clean
waking me up

Then there's nothing
nothing except you
and all your perfect beauty

I love you bird
bird
I love you

I LOVE YOU BIRD

THANK YOU FOR READING THIS BOOK

A DROP OF DEW HOLDS SO MUCH WONDER
IT'S MORE BEAUTIFUL THAN ANY JEWEL
YET MORE TRANSIENT AND FRAGILE AND TRUE

PLEASE TAKE THE TIME TO SEE AND SHARE THE BEAUTY
IN ALL THE SMALL THINGS
I BELIEVE IT IS OUR TRUE WEALTH
TO BEHOLD
IN THIS EVERYDAY MAGIC OF EXISTENCE

APENDIX

POEMS AS SONGS AVAILABLE BY THESE ARTISTS AND ALBUMS

1 THE WINKSTRESS - MOONFLOWERS - COLOURS AND SOUNDS
2 FRIENDS - MOONFLOWERS - COLOURS AND SOUNDS/DONT JUST SIT THERE FLY
3 LETS BUILD A HOUSE - SOLAR MUMUNS - BE IN TOUCH
4 WE NEVER WEAR OUR BODIES - SOLAR MUMUNS - BROKEN WATERS
5 BLACK SWAN - MORNING STAR - THE OPPOSITE IS TRUE/SOLAR MUMUNS - BE IN TOUCH
6 I WILL CALL YOU MY BE FLAME - INVISIBLE PAIR OF HANDS - UNRELEASED
7 I WILL CRY YOUR TEARS - UNRELEASED
8 WOULD YOU LIKE TO FALL APART IN MY ARMS - SOLAR MUMUNS - BE IN TOUCH
9 EVERYTHING COMES THROUGH YOU - PHEONIX FAMILY - MELODIES FOR THE SKY
10 WE WASHED OUR MINDS WITH STARS - PHEONIX FAMILY - MELODIES FOR THE SKY
11 WHERE ARE YOU NOW - PHEONIX FAMILY - MELODIES OF THE SKY
12 KEEPERS OF THE FIRE - MOONFLOWERS - COLOURS AND SOUNDS
13 KEEPERS OF THE FIRE PART 2 MOONFLOWERS - COLOURS AND SOUNDS/MORNING STAR MY PLACE IN THE DUST/GURT LUSH CHOIR
14 I LOVE YOUR EYES - MOONFLOWERS - DONT JUST SIT THERE FLY
15 SO MANY TEARS - MOON FLOWERS - THE LIFE AND DEATH OF LIFE AND DEATH
16 BETWEEN YOUR LOVE AND MY DEATH - SOLAR MUMUNS - BE IN TOUCH
17 DO NOT FEAR THE DARKNESS - ERIF BURNER - DO NOT FEAR THE DARKNESS
18 I HEAR THE WAVES ARE WAITING - MORNING STAR - MY PLACE IN THE DUST
19 SHARE YOUR FOOD - MOONFLOWERS - WHALES TO JUPITER
20 TOO MUCH LOVE - MOONFLOWERS COLOURS AND SOUNDS/MORNING STAR - THE OPPOSITE IS TRUE /ORGANELLES - COVERS AND RESOUNDS
21 JUPITER - MOONFLOWERS - WHALES TO JUPITER
22 LAST LONELY SLEEP - MOONFLOWERS - LIFE AND DEATH / INVISIBLE PAIR OF HANDS - UNRELEASED
23 BIG DISCO IN THE SKY - MOONFLOWERS - BLUE LIFE STRIPES
24 SOFT FIRE - SOLAR MUMUNS - BE IN TOUCH
25 DREAM LOVERS - MOONFLOWERS - WHALES TO JUPITER
26 OH MY DARLING - SOLAR MUMUNS - BROKEN WATERS
27 I DON'T MIND - PHEONIX FAMILY MELODIES FOR THE SKY
28 COLOURS AND SOUNDS - MOONFLOWERS - COLOURS AND SOUNDS
29 SALT BLUE SEA - LURRA URA - UNREALESED
30 I LOVE YOU BIRD - MORNING STAR - THE OPPOSITE IS TRUE (NEWT LOVE)

OTHER BOOKS BY A CONSCIOUS TIDE

due for release

PATHS TO PEACE

an exploration of how to walk closer to peace ,idea's,tools and stratigies to help bring the world closer to peace

THE SEVENTH SENSE

we are mostly aware of our 5 senses and some of our '6th' sense ,this book explores our 7th sense, our sense of relationships,the one sense that rules them all

Printed in Great Britain
by Amazon